Classical
Hungarian Dishes

Boldizsár Horváth

Classical *Hungarian* Dishes

CORVINA

Published by CORVINA
1051 Budapest, Vörösmarty tér 1.

Hungarian text © Boldizsár Horváth, 2001
Translation © Mari Horváth, 2001

Design: Péter Tóth
Photographs: Árpád Patyi
The dishes were prepared by
master chef Péter Korpádi.

ISBN 9 63 13 4988 8
Printed in Hungary, 2001

By way of introduction – Some helpful hints

Traditional Hungarian cooking has always been known for its especially tasty dishes, the secret of which lies in no small measure in the use of ingredients found in abundance in Hungary which are always fresh, tasty, and fragnant, often delivering punch. Hungarian cooks, too, have taken pride of place among the celebrated chefs of the world. Nonetheses, bowing to the requirements of modern, healthy food consumption and the changing tastes and fashions in food, today's recipes call for oil instead of lard and goose fat, and use less bacon and paprika, but always with an eye out to what really counts – a memorable dining eperience.

Hungarian cooks still use paprika, especially when preparing meat dishes, as well as onions, smoked bacon, green peppers, tomatoes and sour cream, which in Hungary tends to be more sour than in some other parts of the world. The "sweet-noble" and *"csemege"* -type paprika can be used in abundance, as it is not hot at all. (In this book, whenever paprika is called for, it is the "sweet-noble" variety.) However, keep in mind that paprika burns easily and turns bitter when added to hot oil, so do not leave on the stove, but immediately add the other ingredients called for by the recipe.

The famous Hungarian *pörkölt* is made by frying lots of finely chopped onion in oil until transparent, adding a sprinkling of paprika, and immediately afterwards, the meat cut into cubes (to prevent the paprika from burning). Stir thoroughly and stew in its own juices. (This type of stewing makes the dish a *pörkölt*.) If the juices are gone, add only a bit of water at a time (or use consommé or wine) to prevent the dish from cooking, and to insure its characteristic good taste.

Paprikás dishes are made from a *pörkölt* base. When the meat is almost done, add sour cream thickened with a bit of flour, stir and let the juices come to the boil. Serve fresh sour cream in a separate bowl.

Another characteristic of many Hungarian dishes is the addition of *roux* or a mixture of sour cream and flour (called *habarás*) as thickening agents.

You will also find desserts calling for *pasta* or *noodles*. The use of pastas for hot desserts, especially as sweets with poppy seeds, walnuts, fruit jellies and jam, is probably peculiar to Hungary – poor men's dishes that have gained wide popularity because they are filling, delicous, and inexpensive to make. Another peculiarity of Hungarian cuisine is the serving of non-sweet pasta, such as cottage cheese noodles, made with bacon bits, as desserts – a nice change from usual sweets. But whichever you choose to finish off your Hungarian meal, good appetite to everyone at your table.

To make a roux, add flour to hot (but not burning-hot) oil or margarine and stir until just light brown. Always dilute the hot roux with a little cold water and cold roux with hot water to prevent lumps. Various seasonings can be added to the roux just before it is ready to be diluted, but be sure to cook the seasonings with the roux for a bit so the flavors can blend. If in doubt, go easy on the flour, because a thick roux will ruin the dish!

To make the traditional Hungarian *habarás*, mix some flour into 2-3 tbsp. of sour cream (or for certain dishes, heavy cream), add a bit of liquid to lighted it and prevent clumps, stir into the still cooking dish and bring to the boil. (You can substitute cornstarch for the flour.)

Note: Unless otherwise indicated, all recipes are for 4 servings.

S t a r t e r s

Hortobágy pancakes
12 pancakes

(Hortobágyi húsos palacsinta)

For the stuffing:
- 1 lb. veal or boned chicken
- 1 tbsp. oil, 1 tsp. flour
- 1 small onion
- 1 tsp. paprika
- salt, pepper
- 1–1 1/2 cups sour cream

For the pancakes:
- 2 eggs, salt
- appr. 7 oz. flour
- 2 tbsp. oil
- 2 cups milk or 1 cup milk and 1 cup soda water (for lighter pancakes)

Wash and dice the meat. Fry the finely chopped or grated onion until transparent, add the meat, and fry for 2 to 3 minutes over high heat, stirring constantly. Take off the fire, sprinkle with paprika, add salt and pepper, cover and simmer over low heat until tender, adding a little water if the dish is too dry. Remove from the pot, leaving the juice for later, and mince or crush with a fork.

To thicken the gravy: combine until smooth 1 tsp. flour and 1 to 2 tbsp. sour cream, add to the gravy, bring to the boil, add the remaining sour cream and stir thoroughly. Add 1 to 2 tbsp. of the thickened gravy to the crushed meat in order to render the meat spreadable.

To make the pancakes: whip the eggs with the milk and oil until smooth, add salt, then stirring constantly, slowly add the flour until the mixture attains the consistency of a heavy creamed soup. Pre-heat a thin-bottomed non-stick pan, pour in a ladleful of the pancake mix, and dipping the pan carefully, distribute the mix evenly. (When cooking the first pancake, add a bit of oil to the pan.) Cook over medium heat (appr. 1 minute) until the pancake separates from the pan when gently shook. Turn around using a flat spatula and cook the other side until light brown. If the dough breaks apart, add a bit more flour, if it is too thick, add a bit of milk. While the pancakes are cooking, stir the dough from time to time to prevent the flour from settling.

Spread the meat stuffing on the pancakes one by one and fold over to make flat "sacks". Place the pancakes in a fireproof dish, pour the remaining gravy mixed with the sour cream on top, and heat in a pre-heated oven.

Tips: To make lighter pancakes, substitute seltzer for half of the milk. Also, you can use heavy cream instead of sour cream, but the pancakes will be softer and will lose some of their characteristic taste.

Fried goose liver

6–8 servings

(Sült libamáj)

1 lb. goose liver (or larger)	*1–2 cloves garlic or 1 onion*
2 cups milk	*(optional)*
salt	*green pepper and tomatoes*
appr. 1 lb. goose fat	*(for decoration)*

Soak the goose liver in lightly salted milk for at least 1 hour. Melt the goose fat, add the liver (without the milk), pour in 1/2 cup water and cook covered over a low heat until the water has evaporated.

Take the liver from the pan, let cool, and slice. If you want to serve the liver cold, place in the frigidaire whole, then cut into paper-thin slices with a hot knife and decorate with green pepper rings and tomato slices. The fat in which the liver was cooked can be served cold on fresh bread or toast, sprinkled with paprika. Fried goose liver is delicious without any other seasoning, though some prefer to add garlic or a small head of red onion while the liver in cooking.

Fried goose liver

Stuffed fried mushrooms

(Töltött rántott gomba)

10–12 large champignon mushrooms	*1 bunch psalt arsley, pepper*
1 tbsp. lemon juice, salt	*1 tsp. bread crumbs*
For the stuffing:	For frying:
1 tbs. oil, 1 egg, salt	*7 oz. flour*
1 small onion	*2 eggs, oil*
1 lb. ground veal	*7 oz. bread crumbs*

Wash (but do not peel) the mushrooms and break off the stems. Chop the stems into small pieces lengthways and set aside. Cook the caps in lightly salted lemon-water for 10 minutes.

Fry the finely chopped onion in oil until transparent, add the ground meat, the mushroom stems, and cook until the liquid has evaporated. Transfer to a large dish, let cool, add the egg, the finely chopped parsley, salt and pepper to taste, and a little bit of the bread crumbs to make a thick stuffing. Wipe dry the cooked mushroom caps, stuff with the veal mixture, and carefully roll first in flour, then the whipped up egg and the bread crumbs. Cook in ample hot oil until golden brown and place on a paper towel to absorb the oil. Serve piping hot with sauce tartare and a small serving of rice (optional).

Note: the stuffing can also be made with chicken. To enhance the flavor, add ham, or use goose liver instead of the veal, but in that case, make sure to reduce the cooking time for the stuffing.

Green peppers stuffed with Liptó cheese spread

(Körözöttel töltött paprika)

4 large, meaty green peppers	*5 oz. butter or margarine*
1 small onion	*1 tsp. mustard, salt, pepper*
small bunch chives	*1 heaping tsp. paprika*
7 oz. curded goat cheese or cottage cheese	*1 tsp. anchovy paste*
	pinch of powdered cumin

Wash, dry and core the green peppers. Peel and mince or grate the onion very fine. Chop up the chives.

Combine the curded goat cheese (or cottage cheese) with the butter thoroughly until almost frothy, add the onion, mustard, paprika, pepper, anchovy paste and cumin, combine thoroughly, then add the chives. Do not salt until you've tasted the spread, for the other ingredients may have enough salt in them. (For a milder spread, omit the onion, but use more chives.)Stuff the peppers with the cheese spread, cover and put in the frigidaire for at least 1 hour. Serve cut into thick slices on a bed of lettuce with toast or fresh bread and tomatoes.

Stuffed tomatoes

(Töltött paradicsom)

8 medium-size tomatoes	1 egg
1 lb. ground chicken meat (breast)	salt
5 oz. mushrooms	pepper
1 bunch parsley	2 oz. butter or margarine
1 tbsp. oil	1 cup sour cream
1 small onion	

Wash the tomatoes. To prepare the tomato cases, cut off the top part near the stem, set aside, carefully squeeze out the inside into a bowl, and set that aside too. Cook the finely chopped onion in the oil until transparent, add the ground meat, the thinly sliced mushrooms, and cook, covered, until the juices are almost gone. Remove from the fire, let cool, then add the raw egg, half of the finely chopped parsley, salt and pepper, and combine thoroughly.

Fill the tomatoes with the stuffing, carefully place in a buttered fireproof dish, put the squeezed-out tomato insides through a sieve, pour on top, sprinkle with sour cream, and cook in a preheated medium oven for appr. 5 to 10 minutes. Serve hot, decorated with the remaining parsley.

Stuffed tomatoes

Salads

Hungarian salad dressing is a breeze to make. It consists of water with vinegar or lemon added to taste, plus a dash of sugar. A bit of salad oil, sour cream or yoghurt are optional, as are the addition of onion, garlic, and various spices. Since Hungarian salad dressing is extremely light, use a lot of it; Hungarians often float the salad ingredients in the dressing.

Potato salad

(Burgonyasaláta)

2 1/4 lbs. waxy potatoes	sugar
1 large onion	vinegar
salt, pepper	1 hard-boiled egg (optional)

Cook the potatoes in their jackets in salted water, then peel and let cool partially. Meanwhile, cut the onion into rings.

To make the salad dressing: add sugar and vinegar to taste to at least 1–1 1/2 cup water. (For this salad dressing, add more sugar and vinegar than usual, otherwise it will taste flat.) Peel and cut the cooled down potatoes into rings, salt to taste, sprinkle with pepper and carefully place into the dressing, alternating potato layers with the onion rings.

Note: prepare this salad at least 2 to 3 hours before serving, so the potatoes can soak up the flavor of the dressing. Adding rings of hard boiled egg on top makes for a special treat.

Tomato salad

(Paradicsomsaláta)

1 lb. medium size tomatoes	1 medium size onion or leek
salt	parsley (for decoration)
pepper	

Dip the tomatoes in boiling water and remove the skin. Cut into rings, lightly sprinkle with salt and pepper. Peel the onion or leek and cut into thin rings. To make the dressing, add vinegar and sugar to taste to 1/2 cup water, then add the onions or leeks and the tomato slices. Refrigerate for at least 1 hour for the flavors to blend, then serve well chilled, sprinkled with chopped parsley.

Bean salad

(Babsaláta)

8–9 oz. large kidney or Lima beans	For 11/2 cup salad dressing:
1 tsp. tarragon	salt, sugar
1 bay leaf, 1 large onion	vinegar, oil

Cook the beans with the tarragon and bay leaf in lightly salted water until tender. Drain and put in a salad bowl.

To prepare the salad dressing: add salt, sugar and vinegar to 1 1/2 cups water with either the sweet or sour taste dominating, and with the addition of a dash of oil. Add the onion cut into very thin rings. Refrigerate for at least 2 to 3 hours, so the flavors can blend.

Tip: you can also add other cooked vegetables such as carrots, parsnips or celery, and top with hard boiled eggs cut into rings.

Cucumber salad with sour cream and garlic

(Fokhagymás uborkasaláta)

2 cucumbers or 3–4 young gherkins (appr. 1 lb.)	1/2 cup sour cream
	vinegar, sugar
salt, pepper, 1 clove garlic	pinch paprika

Wash the cucumbers (peel off the skin only if thick), snip off the ends, cut into thin rings, sprinkle with salt and let stand for 30 minutes.

To prepare the dressing: add the crushed garlic, vinegar and sugar to taste to at least 1/3 cup water. Gently squeeze out the cucumber, add to the dressing in a large bowl and sprinkle the top with the sour cream, pepper and paprika.

Tip: You can disregard the water and use 1/2 cup sour cream instead. For extra garlic flavor, add another clove of crushed garlic. Always serve well chilled.

Cucumber salad with sour cream and garlic

S o u p s

Cabbage soup "Hangover style"

(Korhelyleves)

1 lb. smoked meat	*1 heaping tbs. flour, pepper*
1 1/4 lb. sauerkraut	*1 small stick smoked and spiced*
1 1/2 cup sour cream	*sausage, 1 bay leaf*

Cook the smoked meat in 1 to 1 1/2 qt. water. When half cooked add the bay leaf and the cabbage. (If the cabbage is too sour or too salty, rinse with cold water.) When the cabbage is almost done, add the sausage cut into rings and simmer the soup until ready. Combine the flour and 2–3 tbs. sour cream until smooth, add a bit of water, mix again and stirring constantly, add to the soup to thicken it. Season with a bit of pepper and salt to taste, a dash of lemon juice if not sour enough, bring to the boil and continue cooking a bit longer, then mix in half of the remaining sour cream.

Note: This soup should be soury in taste, because as the name indicates, it serves to settle the stomach after too much drink. Serve the remaining sour cream in a separate bowl.

Fisherman's soup

(Halászlé)

1 lb. small fish	*salt*
8 slices lean carp (or other large fish)	*1 hot green pepper or hot cherry*
2 onions, 1 green pepper	*pepper*
1 tomato, 1 tbs. paprika	

Clean the small fish and cook over low heat with the green pepper and the skinned and quartered tomato in just enough water to cover. Discard the small fish, put the liquid through a sieve and cook the finely chopped onion in the liquid for 30 to 35 minutes. When the onion is very soft, put through a sieve, then put back in the liquid, adding 2 qt. water. Bring to the boil, carefully add the carp slices, the roe (if any), the salt and paprika, and cook, covered, over low heat for appr. 10 to 15 minutes.

Tip: For a spicy soup add the hot green pepper cut into rings or crushed cherry pepper (careful, it is very hot!) towards the end of the cooking time. However, it is best to serve these in a separate bowl, for not everyone likes the very hot taste they impart to the soup.

Serve piping hot.

Note: If you do not have small fish handy, you can use fish bouillon cubes, but the taste will not be the same! Also, for a more substantial soup, you can add soup pasta, which always complements the taste of fish beautifully.

Fisherman's soup

Goulash soup with csipetke

(Gulyásleves csipetkével)

1 lb. pork or beef (thick flank and fil-let ends)	*4 oz. carrots, 4 oz. parsnips*
	pinch of powdered cumin
1 large onion, 1 tbsp. oil	*1 lb. potatoes*
1 tsp. paprika	For the csipetke (soup pasta):
salt, pepper	*3 1/2–4 oz. flour*
1 green pepper, 1 tomato	*1 egg, salt*

Wash, clean and cube the meat. Fry the finely chopped onion in the oil until transparent, take the pot from the fire, sprinkle with paprika, add the meat and cook over high heat for a couple of minutes, stirring constantly. Sprinkle with salt and pepper and cook, covered, over a low flame until the meat is half done. Add the cleaned and quartered carrots and parsnips. Meanwhile, *prepare the csipetke:* make a stiff dough from the flour, egg and salt (do not use water!). Dip your fingers in flour, pinch small fingernail size bits out of the dough, and put aside on a flowered board. (The Hungarian name csipetke means 'small pinched dumplings'.)

Peel the potatoes, cut into small cubes, add the meat and vegetables cooked down to a glaze, mix and cook together for a couple of minutes, then add at least 1 qt. water. Bring to the boil, add the *csipetke* and the green pepper cut into thin rings, the peeled and quartered tomato, salt to taste (a pinch of powdered cumin is optional), and cook over low heat until all the ingredients are tender. Add the csipetke only towards the end of the cooking time, because it is ready in 5–6 minutes.

Tip: For those who like their soup "hot" and spicy, serve with crushed cherry peppers in a separate bowl.

Quick tomato soup

(Paradicsomleves)

1 tbsp. oil	*1 bouillon cube*
1 heaping tbsp. flour	*salt*
1 qt. tomato juice or a small can of tomato purée	*1 tbsp. powdered sugar*
	2 sticks celery

Make a light roux with the oil and flour and add the tomato juice or the tomato purée. (If you use purée, first add a bit of water and stir until smooth, then add enough water to make 1 qt. liquid before stirring into the roux). Stirring constantly, bring to the boil, add the bouillon cube, the celery sticks, the sugar, and continue boiling on a low flame for 10 minutes.

Note: this soup can be made more substantial with the addition of rice which, however, will extend the cooking time. You can also add some green pepper rings for taste, or more sugar, depending on how sweet you like your tomatoes.

Újházy chicken soup

(Újházy tyúkleves)

1 appr. 3 1/2 lb. chicken	*3–4 oz. celeriac*
10–12 peppercorns	*1 small cauliflower*
1 clove garlic, salt	*pinch ginger*
1 small onion	*5 oz. green peas (hulled)*
5 oz. carrots,	*5 oz. mushrooms*
5 oz. parsnips	*2 oz. vermicelli pasta*

Wash and cut up the chicken to your liking and place in a pot with 2 qt. cold water. Add salt and bring to the boil, remove the foam from the top, reduce the heat, add the vegetables, cleaned and cut into matchsticks, the onion (whole), the cauliflower separated into florettes, the ginger, the peppercorns and garlic wrapped in cheese cloth or placed in a tea egg. Continue cooking, covered, over low heat. When the chicken is almost fully cooked, add the mushrooms cut into slices, the green pepper cut into rings, and the green peas. Continue cooking for a few more minutes, then add the pasta and boil for an additional 2 to 3 minutes or until the pasta is ready. Take out the tea egg or cheese cloth, discard the onion and let the soup settle. Serve piping hot.

Tip: If you like lots of vegetables in your soup, add cohlrabi, Brussel sprouds and asparagus.

Chicken ragout soup

(Csirkeraguleves)

1 bunch giblets (wings, neck, legs, liver, etc.)	*1 small cauliflower, 1 tbsp. oil*
	1 small onion, salt
7 oz. carrots	*1 tbsp. flour, 1 clove garlic*
7 oz. parsnips	*8–10 peppercorns*
7 oz. mushrooms	*1 bunch parsley*

Carefully clean and cut up the giblets, removing any extra fat. Clean and dice the vegetables, cut the mushrooms into thin slices, separate the cauliflower into florettes. Heat the oil, add the finely chopped onion, the vegetables, salt to taste and cook for a couple of minutes. Sprinkle with the flour, cook for an additional minute or two, then stirring constantly, add 1 qt. cold water and the peppercorns and garlic wrapped in cheese cloth or put in a tea egg. Add the giblets to the soup, bring to the boil, add more salt to taste (or a bouillon cube) and cook, covered, over low heat until the meat is tender. If you add chicken livers, remember that they need only a couple of minutes of cooking time! Serve sprinkled with finely chopped parsley.

Note: You can use any vegetables of your choice for the soup, including green pepper, tomatoes, celeriac and celery, green peas, kohlrabi and asparagus. The more vegetables you use, the richer the taste.

Bean soup with smoked pig's hocks   6 servings

(Bableves füstölt csülökkel)

5 oz. kidney or haricot beans	*2 tbsp. flour*
1 smoked pig's hocks or other smoked pork (appr. 1 1/2 lb.)	*1–2 cloves garlic*
	1 level tsp. paprika
7 oz. parsnips	*salt*
3 1/2 oz. carrots	*1 cup sour cream*
1 tbsp. oil	*csipetke*

Soak the beans overnight. Cook the smoked pig's hocks (knuckle) in 1 1/2 qt. of water. Taste the cooking liquid after the hocks have boiled for 15 minutes. If the soup is too salty, pour off the liquid and add fresh water. When the hocks are partly tender, add the beans. When the beans are also partly cooked, add the cleaned and quartered vegetables. Cut the bone off the cooked hocks, cut the meat into small serving pieces, and put back in the soup.

To make a roux: stirring constantly, lightly brown the flour in the oil, add the crushed garlic, stir and cook for a very short while, take the pot from the stove, sprinkle with paprika, add at least 1 cup cold water, stir until smooth, and add, stirring, into the soup. Bring to the boil, then continue to simmer for at least 10 minutes.

Bean soup with smoked pig's hocks

Tip: To make this soup into an extra special treat, make it with csipetke (see Goulash soup recipe). Serve with sour cream in a separate bowl, though some people prefer this classic Hungarian soup with a dash of vinegar, or both.

Note: This soup is equally delicious made in a pressure cooker – and much quicker, too!

Hungarian mushroom soup

(Magyaros gombaleves)

1 qt. meat stock (made from bouillon cubes)	*10–11 oz. mushrooms*
	1 tsp. paprika
1 carrot	*pinch of pepper*
1 parsnip	*1 tbsp. flour*
1 tbs. oil	*1 cup sour cream*
1 small onion	*1 bunch parsley*

Make the bouillon with the two cubes and cook the cleaned carrots and parsnips cut into rings until soft.

Meanwhile, grate or chop the onion very fine, chop up the parsley, clean the mushrooms in plenty of water (but do not peel, just remove the stem), and slice.

Braise the onion in the oil, add the mushrooms, braise in its own juices for 5 minutes, sprinkle with the paprika and add the stock.

Combine the flour with 2 to 3 tbsp. of the sour cream until smooth, add the parsley, stir in a bit of water, and stirring constantly, add to the soup to thicken it. Just before serving, add half of the remaining sour cream. Serve the rest in a separate bowl.

Note: This soup can also be made with small galuska dumplings (see Chicken paprikás recipe).

Cold sour cherry soup

(Hideg meggyleves)

1 1/2 lb. fresh or canned sour cherries	*salt*
1 tsp. grated lemon peel	*dash of cinnamon*
1 tsp. lemon juice	*1 cup sour cream*
5 oz. powdered sugar	*1 tbsp. flour*
4 – 5 cloves	*yolk of 1–2 eggs*

Wash the cherries and remove the pits. Cook in 1 qt. water. (If using canned cherries, include the juice.) Add a pinch of salt, the lemon peel, the powdered sugar, the cloves (placed in a tea egg) and the cinnamon. Bring to the boil. Combine the flour with 2 tbsp. sour cream until smooth. Dilute with 1/2 cup water, and stirring constantly, add to the soup. Continue to boil on a medium flame for 5 to 6 minutes, or less if using canned sour cherries. Remove the tea egg and let cool a bit.

In the soup bowl mix the egg yolk(s) into the remaining sour cream, and stirring constantly, pour in the hot soup. Refrigerate for at least 2 hours before serving.

Note: You can substitute heavy cream for some of the sour cream, and add a bit of cognac, provided there are no children at the table.

Cold strawberry soup with heavy cream

(Tejszínes eperleves)

2–3 cloves	*salt*
small stick cinnamon	*1 1/2 cup heavy cream*
juice of 1 lemon	*1 tbsp. flour or corn flour*
2 tbsp. sugar	*1 lb. strawberries*

Cook the cloves and cinnamon (placed in a tea egg), the sugar, a pinch of salt and the lemon juice in 1 qt. of water for appr. 10 to 15 minutes. Combine the flour with 1 to 2 tbsp. heavy cream until smooth, then add the remaining sour cream (this way the mixture will not be lumpy). Stirring constantly, bring to the boil. Clean the strawberries and cut in half, reserving some for decoration. Add to the soup, and continue boiling over medium heat for 3 to 4 minutes. Refrigerate, and serve cold decorated with whipped cream and fresh strawberries.

*Cold strawberry soup
with heavy cream*

F i s h

Carp paprikás

(Pontypaprikás)

2 lb. filéed carp	2 green peppers
salt	1/2 cup sour cream
1 tbsp. oil	1 tbsp. flour
2 oz. smoked bacon	1/2 cup heavy cream
1 large onion	flour
1 tbsp. paprika	

Cut the filéed fish into cubes and salt. Cut the onion very fine, cube the smoked bacon, and render in the oil. Add the onion, fry until transparent, add the green peppers cut into rings, add a bit of water, sprinkle with the paprika, and cook under a lid for 10 to 15 minutes. Add the fish and cook over high heat for an additional 10 to 15 minutes. Combine the sour cream and flour until smooth and stir into the fish. Stirring constantly, add the heavy cream and more salt to taste. The liquid should be substantial and tasty! Serve with simple pasta.

Note: If you decide not to use the smoked bacon, add more oil at the beginning of the cooking time.

Pike in horse radish sauce

(Csuka tormamártásban)

	For the sauce:
1 large carrot	
1 large parsnip	1 stick horse radish
1 small celeriac	1 1/2 oz. butter
1 bay leaf	1 tbsp. flour
salt	1 cup sour cream
1 tbsp. lemon juice	powdered sugar
8 slices pike (or other large fish)	salt
	lemon juice

Clean and cut the vegetables into rings and cook in lightly salted lemon-water with a bay leaf. When the vegetables are nearly tender, carefully add the fish slices and continue cooking over low heat for another 8 to 10 minutes.

To make the horseradish sauce: peel and grate the horse radish and let stand for an hour or place in boiling water in order to reduce the sting. Stir the flour into the melted butter, add 1/2 cup of the fish soup (strained), stir in the grated horse radish, the sour cream, stir again, bring to the boil, and season to taste with sugar and lemon juice.

Carefully remove the fish slices from the soup with a slotted spoon, place on a serving dish, and pour the hot horse radish sauce over the top.

Serve with boiled parsley potatoes.

Layered carp 6–8 servings

(Rácponty)

1 lb. potatoes	1 tsp. paprika
31/2 oz. butter or margarine	5 oz. flour
salt	8–10 slices carp (or other large fish)
3 green peppers	
2 large tomatoes	31/2 oz. smoked bacon
1 large onion	1 cup sour cream

Peel and cut the potatoes into rings and place flat in a buttered fire proof dish. Salt to taste, then layer: add the green peppers cut into rings, the peeled and sliced tomatoes, the onion cut into rings, and crumble pieces of butter (or margarine) on top, reserving some for later. Bake in a medium hot oven for 20 minutes.

Combine the flour and paprika in a bowl. Slice the bacon and place on top of the fish, or skewer in, then gently roll in the flour and paprika mix. Lay on top of the half-baked potatoes, sprinkle with the sour cream, crumble the remainder of the butter (or margarine) on top, put in the oven and continue baking for appr. 30 minutes or until the top is crisp and light brown. Serve with boiled potatoes or flat pasta.

Braised pike in wine sauce

(Párolt csuka bormártásban)

8 big slices of pike (appr. 1²/3 lbs.)	*7 oz. mushrooms*
	salt, pepper
3³/4–4 oz. butter	*1¹/2–2 cups dry white wine*
1 onion	*flour*

Place the fish slices in a buttered non-stick pan. Salt to taste, add the finely chopped or sliced onion and the sliced mushrooms, pepper to taste, add the white wine and cook over low heat. Carefully lift the fish slices out of the pan, set aside and keep warm.

To thicken the gravy in the pan: combine the remaining butter with the flour, and stirring constantly, add to the gravy, a little at a time. Bring to the boil, salt to taste, and pour over the fish. Serve with boiled parsley potatoes.

Paprikás pike-perch

(Fogasszeletek paprikásan)

slices pike-perch	*pepper*
salt	*2 green peppers*
2 oz. butter	*1 large tomato*
1 tbsp. oil	*1/2 cup sour cream*
1 small onion	*1/2 cup heavy cream*
1 tsp. paprika	*81 tbsp. flour*

Sprinkle the fish slices with salt and brown on both sides in the butter. Combine the flour and sour cream until smooth, stir in the heavy cream, add to the fish, bring to the boil, cover and continue cooking over low heat for a couple of minutes, making sure the fish slices do not fall apart. (Do not overcook!)

In a separate pan fry the finely chopped or grated onion until transparent over low heat, sprinkle with paprika, add the green pepper cut into slices, the peeled tomato cut into chunks, salt and pepper to taste and stew until the vegetables are soft. Carefully place the fish slices with the sauce on a serving dish and pour the vegetables over the fish. Serve with boiled potatoes or flat pasta.

Balaton style pike-perch

(Balatoni fogas)

4 pcs. (1 lb.) pike-perch	*1 tsp. paprika*
salt	*oil, lemon*
5 oz. flour	*lettuce leaves*

Carefully clean and gut the fish, rinse in cold water and wipe dry. Salt and score each side perpendicularly to the spine, leaving 1/2 in. between the scorings so the fish will fry evenly. Stir the paprika into the flour, then carefully turn the fish in the mixture. Fry in a pan which will make the fish turn up to form a half-moon shape (or try turning the ends up yourself, by tying the head and tail together).

Fry the fish in the hot oil on both sides until very crispy. Place on a kitchen towel to absorb the excess oil, and serve on a bed of lettuce leaves, decorated with lemon slices. Serve piping hot with boiled and buttered potatoes and sauce tartare.

Note: This dish is good only when freshly made!

Pike-perch in mushroom sauce

(Fogasszeletek gombamártással)

8 slices pike-perch (or other big fish)

salt

3 1/2 oz. butter

1 lb. mushrooms

1 tsp. cornstarch

1/2 cup heavy cream

Slightly salt the fish slices and fry in the hot butter on both sides until red. Carefully remove the fish from the pan, set aside, and keep warm.

To make the mushroom sauce: clean and slice the mushrooms and fry in the remaining gravy, then cover and continue cooking in its own juices until tender. Reduce the liquid if it is too watery, sprinkle with the cornstarch (or a bit of flour), add the heavy cream, stir and bring to the boil, then pour over the fish. Serve piping hot with boiled potatoes or flat pasta.

Poultry and Meats

Stuffed chicken

(Töltött csirke)

oil for baking	3 chicken livers
1 large chicken	5 oz. mushrooms
salt, pepper	2 tbs. oil
pinch marjoram	1 small onion
For the stuffing:	salt, pepper
2 rolls	1 egg
1¹/₂ cups milk	1 bunch parsley

Stuffed chicken

To make the stuffing: soak the rolls in the milk, dice the carefully cleaned liver and the mushrooms. Fry the finely chopped or grated onion in 1 tbsp. oil until transparent, then add the mushrooms. Cover and stew in its own juices. When most of the liquid has evaporated, add the liver, continue frying for a minute or two, spoon into a large bowl, and let cool. Add the squeezed-out rolls, the egg, the finely chopped parsley, salt and pepper, and combine thoroughly.

Clean the chicken, salt and pepper to taste, sprinkle with marjoram and stuff the inside with the mushroom and liver stuffing. Close the opening with meat skewers. Place the chicken in a baking dish or casserole, sprinkle with the remaining 1 tbsp. oil, add a little water and cover. Cook in a medium hot pre-heated oven for appr. 30 minutes. Remove the lid and bake, basting with its own juices, until crisp.

Serve with potato purée or parsley potatoes, and cucumber salad.

Chicken paprikás with galuska dumplings

Chicken paprikás with galuska dumplings

(Paprikáscsirke galuskával)

1 large or 2 smaller chicken	*1 to 1 1/2 cups sour cream*
1 tbsp. oil	*1 heaping tsp. flour*
2 onions	For the galuska:
1 tbsp. paprika	*2 eggs*
1 green pepper	*salt*
1 large tomato	*10–11 oz. flour*
salt, pepper	*1 tbsp. oil*

Clean and cut up the chicken to your liking. Fry the finely chopped or grated onion in the oil until transparent. Take the pan from the fire, sprinkle with paprika, put back on the stove, add the chicken pieces, the green pepper cut into rings, the peeled and quartered tomato, salt, pepper, cover, and stew over low heat until the chicken is tender. (If the chicken does not produce sufficient juice for stewing, add a little water, but only a little at a time as needed!)

Combine the flour and 2 to 3 tbsp. sour cream until smooth and add to the chicken. Stirring constantly, bring to the boil, making sure that the liquid is substantial and thick (though not too thick!). Stir in half the remaining sour cream, retaining the other half in a bowl for serving fresh with the chicken paprikás.

To make the galuska dumplings, the traditional accompaniment to chicken paprikás: beat the 2 eggs with a pinch of salt, stir in the flour, the oil, and enough water to make a soft batter. Boil ample salted water in a large pot and using either a dumpling strainer or a dampened chopping board and a wet knife, "mince" small pieces of batter into the boiling water. Simmer until the galuska comes to the surface, remove with a slotted spoon, quickly rinse in cold water and place in a bowl with a bit of hot oil. Stir and keep warm.

Serve the chicken paprikás piping hot, decorated with green pepper rings.

Chicken legs with grapes

(Szőlős csirkecombok)

8 small (or 4–5 large) chicken legs	*2 oz. butter*
1 pinch dried basil	*1 lb. white and red seedless grapes*
1 pinch dried thyme	*1/2 cup dry white wine*
salt	*1/4 cup heavy cream*
pepper	

Clean the chicken, salt and season with the basil and thyme and cook in the butter until crispy red. Add the wine and the juice of 1/3 of the grapes, cover, and cook over low heat until the chicken is tender. Add the heavy cream and bring to the boil.

Stew the remainder of the grapes in a little butter. Remove the chicken legs from the cooking gravy, arrange on a serving dish, and place the hot stewed grapes around the meat. Serve the cooking gravy piping hot in a separate bowl. Steamed rice or tomato purée go well with chicken dish.

Chicken legs with grapes

Goose giblets with rice

(Rizses libaaprólék)

1 bunch goose giblets (appr. 2 1/4 lbs.)	salt, pepper
1 tbsp. oil	1–2 bouillon cubes
1 large onion	10–11 oz. rice
1–2 cloves garlic	1–2 green peppers
1 tsp. paprika	1–2 tomatoes

Carefully clean the giblets and wash in plenty of water. Cut into desired pieces. Fry the finely chopped onion in half the oil until transparent, add the crushed garlic, the paprika, and immediately add a bit of water. Add the giblets, salt and pepper to taste, and braise under a lid until the giblets are nearly done. Add enough water to cover, crumble 1 or 2 bouillon cubes over it – remember, the cubes contain salt!), add the rice, first party fried in the remainder of the oil, the green pepper(s) cut into large pieces, and the peeled tomatoes cut into chunks. Cover, and continue cooking over low heat until the rice and the giblets are both done.

Serve with mixed pickles.

Ground breast of goose   6 servings

(Vagdalt libamell)

1 breast of goose (without the fat, appr. 2 1/4 lbs. with the bone)	1–2 cloves garlic
10–11 oz. ground pork	pepper
2 rolls	marjoram
1/2 cup milk	1 egg
1 medium onion	salt
	oil

Bone the breast of goose, put through a grinder, place in a large mixing bowl and add the ground pork. Soak the rolls in milk, squeeze out and add to the ground meat. Season with the crushed garlic cloves, a pinch of marjoram, add the egg, salt and pepper to taste, and combine thoroughly.

Place the meat back on the breast bone, shaping it carefully (it should look the way it did before the breast was boned), and place in a rectangular fire proof dish. Heat the oil, pour over the breast, pour a bit of water in the pan, cover, and cook in a preheated oven for appr. 30 minutes. Remove the cover, and basting from time to time, cook the meat until crispy red on top. If the gravy evaporates during cooking time, add a bit more water as needed.

Serve with potato purée or fried onion potatoes.

Stuffed turkey breast Bakony style

(Bakonyi töltött pulykamell)

1 3/4 lbs. turkey breast (boned)	**For baking:**
rosemary, thyme	2 tbsp. oil
For the stuffing:	2 oz. meaty bacon
1/2 lbs. ground pork	**For the sauce:**
2 oz. meaty bacon	10–11 oz. mushrooms
1 clove garlic	1/2 cup sour cream
1 egg	1/2 cup heavy cream
salt, pepper	1 tbsp. flour
1 level tsp. paprika	

With a long, sharp knife make a deep hole in the middle of the turkey breast, carefully pry loose, and sprinkle inside and out with a bit of marjoram, thyme, and salt.

To make the stuffing: add the crushed garlic to the ground pork, the diced meaty bacon, the egg, salt and pepper, sprinkle with paprika, and combine thoroughly.

Stuff the turkey breast with the mixture and close the openings with skewers. (If the stuffing is too soft, add some bread crumbs.)

Fry the 2 oz. meaty bacon in the oil, add and sauté the finely chopped onion until transparent, and quick grown the turkey on both sides. Add appr. 1/2 cup water and cook under a lid until tender. When the turkey is done, carefully remove from the pan, set aside, and keep warm.

To make the mushroom sauce: place the cleaned and sliced mushrooms in the cooking liquid and stew, covered, over low heat until the gravy is rendered down to the fat. Combine 2 to 3 tbs. sour cream and the flour until smooth, add the remaining sour cream and the heavy cream, and stir into the mushroom sauce. Bring to the boil and keep warm.

Cut the stuffed turkey breast into thick slices, pour some of the hot mushroom sauce over it, and serve the rest in a separate bowl.

Serve with rice, potatoes, or galuska dumplings *(see Chicken paprikás recipe)*.

Veal pörkölt

(Borjúpörkölt)

2 lb. leg or lean breast or shoulder	salt
	pepper
1 large onion	1 green pepper
2 tbsp. oil	1 tomato
1 tsp. paprika	

Veal pörkölt

Cut the meat into small cubes. Finely chop the onion and sauté in the oil until transparent. Reduce the heat, add the paprika, then immediately the meat to prevent the paprika from burning and turning bitter. Salt to taste and brown, stirring frequently.

When the meat is browned, add a small amount of water or stock. Cover the pot and simmer, stirring occasionally. Add more liquid as needed, but very sparingly; for full flavor, the meat should be browned, not cooked. When the meat is partly tender, add the green pepper cut into rings and the peeled tomato cut into chunks. Ssimmer until tender, remove the lid and cook until only a thick gravy remains. (You may want to thin it with a little water or red wine.) Serve with galuska dumplings (*see Chicken paprikás recipe*).

Note: Pork and beef stew (called *pörkölt*, it being a kind of stew cooked in its own juices) is made the same way, only the cooking time is slightly longer.

Veal medallions in white wine

(*Részeges borjútokány*)

1 1/2 lbs. veal	pepper
1 onion	pinch marjoram
1 tbsp. oil or 1 oz. butter	1/2 cup white wine
1 clove garlic	1/2 cup heavy cream
salt	1 level tbsp. flour or cornstarch

Cut the meat into medallions. Finely chop the onion and sauté in the oil or butter until transparent. Add the meat and cook over high heat for 2 to 3 minutes, until pink. Add salt, pepper and marjoram to taste, add the crushed garlic clove, continue to brown for another 1 to 2 minutes, add the white wine and stew, covered, over low heat until tender.

Mix together the heavy cream and flour until smooth, and slowly stir into the meat gravy to thicken. Serve with rice, boiled potatoes or potato purée.

Stuffed breast of veal

(*Töltött borjúszegy*)

1 3/4 lbs. breast of veal	7 oz. mushrooms
salt, pepper	2–3 chicken livers
For the stuffing:	1 egg
2 rolls	1 bunch parsley
1 1/2 cup milk	salt, pepper
2 tbsp. oil	1 clove garlic
2 small onions	oil (for frying)

Wash and pat the meat dry. With a sharp knife, made a slit in the middle to make a small "pocket", then carefully enlarge the "pocket" for the stuffing. Salt and pepper to taste.

To make the stuffing: soak the rolls in milk. Fry one finely chopped onion in 1 tbsp. oil, add the chopped mushrooms, cook over medium heat until only the oil remains, add the chicken livers cut into small pieces, and continue cooking for another 1 to 2 minutes.

Transfer the stuffing into a large bowl, let cool, add the egg, the finely chopped parsley, the well squeezed out rolls, salt and pepper to taste, and work loosely together.

Stuff the breast of veal with the stuffing and sew the opening together. Lay in a fireproof dish, sprinkle with a bit of hot oil, add 1/2 cup water, the remaining onion, and the garlic. Bake in a preheated medium oven until tender. Cover the dish with a lid or aluminum foil. After appr. 40 minutes, remove the cover and bake until crispy brown. Serve with potato purée, buttered potatoes, or rice.

Hungarian escalopes of veal

(Magyaros bélszínérmék)

2 lb. tenderloin	1 clove garlic
salt, pepper	1 tsp. paprika
2 tbsp. oil	1 lb. green peppers
1 small onion	1/2 lb. tomatoes

Wash and trim the veal and cut into small slices, 3 per serving. *To marinade:* 3 to 4 days before cooking, dip in oil, sprinkle with pepper, wrap in aluminum foil and place in the frigidaire.

In a fireproof dish sauté the finely chopped onion in 1 tbsp. oil until transparent, add the crushed garlic, sprinkle with paprika, add the green pepper cut into pieces, continue lightly browning, add the peeled and quartered tomatoes, salt to taste, and cook until tender.

In a non-stick pan brown the veal in the remaining oil, about 2 to 3 minutes on each side. Lay the escalopes on top of the vegetable stew. Serve piping hot accompanied by rice or parsley potatoes.

Veal stew in red wine

(Vörösboros marhapörkölt)

2 lbs. juicy veal (leg or lean breast or shoulder)	*salt*
	pepper
2–3 tbsp. oil	*1 cup dry red wine*
2 onions	*1 green pepper*
1 tbsp. paprika	*1 small tomato*

Cut the meat into cubes. Finely chop the onion and sauté in the oil until transparent, sprinkle with paprika, and immediately add the meat. Stirring constantly, brown over high heat for a couple of minutes. Salt and pepper to taste and stew, covered, in its own juices over medium heat until tender. If the juices are gone, add some red wine, but only a bit at a time, so that the meat will not cook, just stew. When it is almost tender, add the de-seeded green pepper, cut into rings and the skinned and quartered tomato. Continue cooking until the gravy thickens, otherwise this Hungarian-type stew will not be authentic!

Serve with galuska dumplings *(see Chicken paprikás recipe)* or boiled potatoes.

Escalopes of veal Budapest style

(Bélszín Budapest módra)

4 slices fillet of veal (appr. 2 lbs.)	*1 onion*
mustard	*1 level tsp. paprika*
pepper for the marinade	*1 tbsp. tomato purée*
2/3–1 lb. bone (veal or pork, chopped into small pieces)	*3–4 oz. smoked meaty bacon*
or use 1–2 bouillon cubes	*7 oz. goose liver (or chicken liver)*
salt	*7 oz. mushrooms*
	2 green peppers
3 tbs. oil	*5 oz. green peas (fresh or canned)*

To marinade the veal slices for 3 to 4 days before cooking: spread thinly with oil, spread with mustard, sprinkle with pepper, and placing the slices one on top of the other, wrap in aluminum foil and place in the frigidaire.

Sauté the finely chopped onion in 1 tbsp. oil until transparent, sprinkle with the paprika, add the tomato purée, stir, add the carefully washed and cleaned bones, salt to taste, add enough water to cover, and cook over low heat for 30-40 minutes, then put the bouillon through a sieve.

Meanwhile, *prepare the ragout:* cut the bacon, the mushrooms, the liver and green peppers into small cubes. Cook the bacon in a little oil until transparent, then add the mushroom, followed by the green pepper. When the cooking liquid has evaporated, add the liver. Continue frying for a few moments, add the sieved bouillon, bring to the boil, and add more salt to taste. Be sure not to add too much bouillon, lest the veal will be too soupy. Cook the green peas separately until tender.

When the above ingredients are ready, fry the veal slices in hot oil on both sides until nice and pink (do not overcook!), arrange the ragout on top, and sprinkle with the green peas. Serve with potatoes or rice.

Pan-fried rostélyos

(Serpenyős rostélyos)

4 slices boned sirloin of beef (appr. 1³/4 lb.)	*1 large onion*
salt	*1 tbsp. paprika*
pepper	*dash of powdered cumin*
1 whole garlic (crushed)	*1 lb. potatoes*
2 tbsp. oil	*1 green pepper*
	1 small tomato

Score the meat slices all around, salt and pepper to taste, then spread the crushed garlic on top. Cook the finely chopped onion in the oil, add the meat, sprinkle with paprika, a dash of cumin (optional) and stew in its own juice, covered, over low heat, until almost tender. If needed, add water, but only a little at a time, in order to insure that the flavor is not lost.

Meanwhile, peel the potatoes and cut into lengthways pieces, as for French fries. Add to the meat, add a bit of water and more salt to taste, the green pepper cut into rings, and the peeled and chopped-up tomato. Continue cooking over low heat for appr. 15 to 20 minutes. Make sure the cooking gravy is thick!

Serve hot with boiled potatoes or galuska dumplings *(see Chicken paprikás recipe)*.

Roast suckling pig with stewed cabbage

(Malacsült párolt káposztával)   8–10 servings

1 piglet (appr. 7 lbs.)	For the stewed cabbage:
salt, pepper	*1 3/4–2 lbs. cabbage*
marjoram, thyme	*2 tbsp. oil*
1 bottle of beer	*1 heaping tsp. sugar*
5 oz. smoked bacon	*1 tsp. vinegar*
oil (for frying)	*salt*
1 onion, 1–2 cloves garlic	*ground cumin*

Clean and wipe the piglet thoroughly inside and out. Salt and pepper the inside, sprinkle generously with marjoram and thyme and rub the back with bacon slices soaked in beer. (Repeat this procedure several times while baking, it will render the skin golden brown and crisp!) Place the piglet in a large pan, add the oil and appr. 1 cup water, the onion cut in half, the garlic cloves, and bake, covered, in a medium oven for appr. 2 hours. If the cooking juices evaporate before the piglet is tender, add a bit of water at a time as needed. When the piglet is tender, remove the cover and continue baking in a hot oven until golden brown and crisp.

In the meanwhile, *prepare the stewed cabbage:* shred the cabbage, sprinkle with salt and let stand for appr. 30 minutes, then squeeze out. Heat the oil, brown the sugar in the oil, add the cabbage, the vinegar, salt and ground cumin, and stir thoroughly. Cover and cook over low heat. Adding a little water at a time as needed, stirring occasionally, cook until most of the cooking juice is gone.

Note: If you don't like the taste of cumin in the cabbage, you can leave it out. Also, you can substitute white wine or champagne for the water lost during the cooking time.

Knuckle of ham Hungarian style

(Csülök pékné módra)

2 medium-size or 4 small raw	*pepper*
knuckle of ham (pork) or veal	*2–3 tbsp. oil*
(appr. 3 lbs. with bone)	*2 lbs. potatoes*
salt	*2 large onions*

Clean the knuckle, turn in the hot oil, salt and pepper to taste, add water, cover and cook over low heat until tender. (To reduce cooking time, use a pressure cooker!) When the knuckle is tender, remove the bone and place in a large fireproof dish along with the left-over cooking juices, add the peeled, salted potatoes cut into rings, the onions cut into rings, and bake in a preheated medium oven until crisp. Be sure to turn the potatoes round a couple of times and to baste the knuckle! Serve with mixed pickles.

Pork with potatoes

(Brassói aprópecsenye)

1 lb. pork (or veal) fillets	*oil for frying the potatoes*
1 onion	*1 tbsp. oil for frying the meat*
3 cloves garlic	*1 heaping tsp. paprika*
1 green pepper	*marjoram*
1 lb. potatoes	*salt, pepper*

Cut the meat into thin strips, chop the onion and crush the garlic, cut the green pepper into rings.

Peel the potatoes, cut into julienne slices, fry in plenty of hot oil until light brown, and lay on a paper towel to soak up the extra oil.

In a separate pan heat the 1 tbsp. oil, add the meat and cook over high heat for 2-3 minutes, lower the heat, add the onion, the crushed garlic and the green pepper, continue cooking for another 4 to 5 minutes, sprinkle with paprika, marjoram, salt and a liberal amount of pepper. Stirring constantly, continue frying for a bit longer, add the fried potatoes, continue heating till the potatoes are hot, and serve at once with mixed pickles.

Note: Instead of oil, you can fry the meat in the rendered fat of smoked bacon.

Csabai pork chops 6–8 servings
(Csabai sertéskaraj)

1 boned side of pork (or veal), appr. 1 1/2 lbs.	*pepper*
	oil for frying
7 oz. smoked sausage (the small, hard variety)	*2–3 onions*
	2 cloves garlic
salt	

Using a sharp knife, made a slit lengthways in the middle of the pork, then gently ease the hole open and place the smoked sausage inside. Place the meat in a fireproof dish, salt and pepper to taste, sprinkle with hot oil, add 1/2 cup water, the onions and garlic, cover and bake in a medium oven until tender (appr. 1 hour). Remove the lid, increase the heat, and basting frequently, bake until the meat is golden brown. Remove from the oven, let stand a bit, then cut into finger-thick slices, arrange on a serving dish, and pour the hot cooking gravy in a smaller dish for serving separately. Serve with potato purée, baked potatoes or rice.

Note: You can substitute a good dry white wine for the water. If serving cold, cut into thinner slices.

Csikós tokány

1 1/2 lbs. lean pork	*pepper*
4 oz. smoked bacon	*2 green peppers*
1 large onion	*1 tomato*
1 tsp. paprika	*1/2 cup sour cream*
salt	*1 heaping tsp. flour*

Clean and cut the meat into finger-thick slices. Cut the bacon into strips, make slits in the skin and fry until pink, remove from the fat and set aside.

Fry the thinly sliced onion in the bacon fat until transparent, sprinkle with the paprika, immediately add the meat and stir. Salt and pepper to taste and cook, covered, in its own juices until almost tender. Add the green peppers cut into rings and

Csabai pork chops

the tomato, skinned and quartered, and continue cooking until the meat is tender and only the fatty juices remain in the pan (or almost just). Combine the flour with 1 to 2 tbsp. sour cream until smooth, add a little water, and stir into the hot meat dish. Just before serving, add the remaining sour cream and place the fried bacon slices on top. Serve with galuska *(see Chicken paprikás recipe)*, boiled rice or boiled potatoes.

Note: This dish can also be made from beef, but in that case, it will take longer to cook.

Vasi pecsenye

1–1 1/2 cups milk	*8 small slices leg of pork or lean veal*
salt, pepper	*(appr. 1 3/4 lbs.)*
3 cloves garlic	*oil for frying*

*A*dd salt and pepper to the milk, followed by the crushed garlic and the meat slices and marinade for 2 to 3 hours, or overnight. Remove the meat from the milk, wipe or drip dry, and fry in a small amount of oil on both sides to the preferred state of doneness. Serve with potato purée and stewed vegetables.

Transylvanian mixed grill
(Erdélyi fatányéros)

4 small slices pork chops	*1 lb. potatoes for French fries*
4 small slices veal chops	*oil for frying the potatoes*
4 small slices sirloin steak	*mixed pickles and lettuce leaves for*
salt	*decoration*
pepper	*tomato*
4 oz. smoked bacon	*green pepper*
2 tbsp. oil	*pinch of paprika*
4 oz. flour	

*C*arefully clean the meat slices, pound gently, salt and pepper to taste. Cut the bacon into four equal slices, score the skin and fry, set aside and keep warm. Turn the meat slices in the flour and fry in hot oil on both sides until red. Meanwhile, prepare the French fries in a separate pan, making sure that they are done at the same time as the meat.

Place the French fries in the middle of a large wooden platter and arrange the meat around it. Decorate the edge of the platter with the lettuce leaves, the mixed pickles and the tomato and green pepper cut into rings, score the fried bacon into the shape of a cock's comb, sprinkle with paprika, and arrange on top of the meat.

Note: One slice of each meat makes one portion.

Pork with mushrooms

(Gombás flekken)

8 small slices lean pork (or veal)	*2 tbsp. oil*
salt	*1 lb. mushrooms*
pepper	*1 tbsp. grated onion*
3¹/2 oz. flour	*1 cup sour cream*
cornstarch	*1/4 cup heavy cream*

Sprinkle the meat slices with salt and pepper and turn in the flour. Heat the oil, add the meat, and fry until pink on both sides.

Clean the mushrooms, cut into slices, and add to the meat. Cook, covered, over medium heat until the meat is tender (appr. 15 minutes). Take out the meat and continue cooking the mushrooms until the liquid evaporates, add the heavy cream, half of the sour cream, and mix thoroughly. (If the gravy is too thin, add a bit of cornstarch). Put the meat back in the pan and cook with the mushrooms for a couple of minutes longer. Serve with rice or potatoes and the remaining sour cream in a separate bowl.

Highwayman's treat on a spit

(Rablóhús nyárson)

7 oz. sirloin steak	2 cloves crushed garlic
7 oz. lean pork	7 oz. smoked bacon
7 oz. veal	2 onions
salt, pepper	10 oz. mushrooms

Cut the meat into medallions or cubes of equal size, pound gently, salt and pepper to taste, and brush with the crushed garlic. Cut the bacon into pieces about the same size as the meat. Cut the onion into thick slices, clean the mushrooms and break off and discard the stems. Skewer the ingredients onto small spits in the following order: mushroom, onion, bacon, meat (only one kind at a time), then mushroom again and so on. Fry the spits in a microwave oven with a rotary, or use the oven, arranging the spits over a deep baking pan, brushing them with cooking oil, then grill, turning frequently, until the meat is nice and crisp. Serve with fried potatoes and mixed pickles.

Note: This basic recipe can be varied at will with the addition of various vegetables, such as green peppers and potatoes, or the substitution of sausage for some of the meat.

Braised liver

(Pirított máj)

1¹/4 lb. calf's, chicken or pork liver	salt
1 onion	pepper
1 tbsp. oil	1 green pepper
1 tsp. paprika	

Wash the liver and wipe dry, then cut into finger-length strips. Heat the oil in a pan and add the finely chopped onion. Sauté the onion until transparent. Remove from the heat, stir in the paprika, put back on the stove, immediately add the liver and the de-seeded green pepper cut into thin rings. Sprinkle with pepper and fry over high heat for a couple of minutes, stirring all the time. Do not add salt until the liver is ready! Chicken liver takes less time to cook that either calf or pork liver, but whichever type you use, do not overcook, or it will turn tough.

Serve with boiled potatoes and mixed pickles.

Casseroles

Stuffed cabbage

(Töltött káposzta)

1/2 lb. smoked lean pork chops	For the stuffing:
2 lbs. sour cabbage (shredded)	2 oz. rice
4 oz. smoked bacon	1 1/4 lb. ground lean pork
1 onion, 2 tsp. paprika	1 clove garlic
5 oz. paprika sausage	1 egg
1–2 bay leaf	salt
1–1 1/2 cups sour cream	pepper
1 tbsp. flour	8–10 soured cabbage leaves

Cook the meat in appr. 1 quart of water until half done. Cook the rice separately until half done.

To prepare the stuffing: combine the ground meat, the drained rice, the crushed garlic, the egg, salt and pepper, and blend well together. Place some stuffing on each cabbage leaf and roll up, tucking the ends in so the leaves won't open. Wet your hands and shape the remaining stuffing into balls.

In a large pot fry the smoked bacon cut into small cubes until the fat is rendered, add the finely chopped onion and sauté until transparent, sprinkle with paprika, add half of the sour cabbage (if it's too sour or salty, run cold water through it first), followed by the stuffed cabbage leaves and meat balls, and finally, the rest of the sour cabbage. Cut the sausage into rings and place on top, add the bay leaf and the smoked pork chops along with the cooking liquid. (If the liquid is too salty, add some water, but just enough to cover the cabbage half-way. Cover and cook over low heat until tender.

Remove the stuffed cabbage leaves and the smoked meat with a slotted spoon and set aside. Combine the flour with 2-3 tbsp. sour cream until smooth, add a little water, stir again, and add to the cabbage, stirring all the time. Bring to the boil, continue boiling for at least 5 minutes, put back the stuffed cabbage leaves, the smoked meat, and bring to the boil once again. Before serving, sprinkle with half of the left-over sour cream; serve the other half in a separate dish on the side.

Note: This dish can also be made with frankfurters instead of the sausage, and you can substitute oil for the smoked bacon, but the taste will not be the same. On the other hand, stuffed cabbage is even better when reheated.

Stuffed peppers

(Töltött paprika)

2 oz. rice	1 tbsp. oil
8 fleshy bell peppers	2 tbsp. flour
1 lb. ground pork	7 oz. tomato purée or 1 qt. tomato
1 clove garlic	juice
1 egg	1 heaping tbsp. powdered sugar
salt	1–2 sticks celery
pepper	

Cook the rice until half done in lightly salted water. Wash and core the peppers. Place the ground meat in a bowl, add the crushed garlic, the drained rice, the egg, salt and pepper to taste, and work thoroughly together. Stuff the peppers with the mixture. Make small meat balls from the remaining stuffing.

In a large non-stick pan prepare a roux with the oil and flour, cooking the flour until light brown, then quickly add 1 1/3 cup water, stirring constantly until smooth. Add the tomato purée and enough water to make appr. 1 quart of liquid (or just use tomato juice). Stir well, add salt and the sugar, the stuffed peppers and meat balls, and

the celery stick. Stirring frequently, bring to the boil, then continue cooking over very low heat until done (appr. 30 to 40 minutes). Add more sugar to taste, or use one or two hot peppers if you want to give this dish a "kick". Serve hot with boiled potatoes.

Layered Savoy cabbage

6 servings

(Rakott kel)

1 head Savoy cabbage (appr. 2¹/2 lbs.)	1¹/4 lb. lean ground pork
	salt
2 oz. rice	pepper
1 tbsp. oil	2 oz. butter or margarine
1 onion	1 ¹/2 cups sour cream
1 clove garlic	4 oz. smoked bacon

Cook the cabbage and the rice separately in lightly salted water until half done. Drain. Set aside a couple of large cabbage leaves. Sauté the onion in the oil until transparent, add the crushed garlic and the ground meat, salt and pepper to taste, combine thoroughly, and stew, covered, in its own juices until half done. Add the pre-cooked rice.

Line the bottom of a fireproof dish with half of the thinly sliced bacon, add a layer of cabbage, a layer of ground meat, crumble a bit of the butter or margarine on top, sprinkle with sour cream, add another layer of cabbage and so on until all the ingredients are used up. Cover the top with the large cabbage leaves, sprinkle the remaining sour cream on top, cover with the left-over bacon slices, and bake in a medium pre-heated oven for appr. 35 to 40 minutes. If you like your dishes well seasoned, add more onion and 1 tsp. paprika to the ground meat.

Note: For a simplified version of this dish, you can leave out the bacon and line the fireproof dish with butter or margarine, and also crumble butter on the top instead of the bacon slices. For this simplified version, though, you will need about 4 oz. of butter.

Stuffed squash with dill sauce

(Töltött tök kapormártással)

2 young squash (appr. 2–2 1/4 lbs.)	*2 oz. butter*
salt	*1/2 cup consommé (or use*
1 tbsp. vinegar	*a bouillon cube)*
1 tbsp. oil	For the dill sauce:
1 onion	*1 large bunch dill*
1 lb. ground pork	*1 1/2 oz. butter*
pepper	*1 tbsp. flour*
1 garlic	*1–1 1/2 cups sour cream*
2 oz. rice	*sugar*
1 egg	*vinegar or lemon juice*

Peel the squash (vegetable marrow), cut in half and scrape out the seeds. Cook in lightly salted vinegar water for 10 minutes, lift out, and put the liquid aside. Sauté the finely chopped onion in the oil until transparent, add the ground meat, salt and pepper to taste, add the crushed garlic, and stirring frequently, cook until the cooking liquid is gone.

Cook the rice in lightly salted water, pour the whole thing into a sieve to get rid of any extra water in the rice, add to the ground meat, and when the meat has cooled down, add the egg and combine.

Pile the ground meat inside the squash, place in a fireproof dish, crumble the butter on top, pour 1/2 cup consommé at the bottom, and bake in a medium oven for 25–30 minutes.

To prepare the dill sauce: chop the dill very fine. Prepare a light roux from the butter and flour, stir in the dill, and continue cooking for a very short time. Add the cooking liquid from the squash, but make sure not to dilute the roux too much, because you will still have to add sour cream. Season with salt and sugar to taste, add a bit of vinegar or lemon juice, boil for 5 minutes, then stir in the sour cream and adjust the seasoning.

Pour some of the dill sauce over the squash. Serve the rest separately in a bowl with rice or boiled potatoes.

Note: to make this dish even more tasty, use ground *pörkölt (see Veal pörkölt recipe)* for the stuffing.

Stuffed kohlrabi

(Töltött karalábé)

10 tender kohlrabi	1 small onion
1 lb. lean ground pork or veal	salt, white pepper
1 egg	1 tbsp. flour
2 oz. rice	1–1^{1}/2 cup sour cream
1 tbsp. oil	1 bunch parsley

Peel the kohlrabi. Scoop out the centers of 8 kohlrabi, chop up the scooped-out parts and set aside. Cut the remaining 2 kohlrabi into small pieces lengthways.

Cook the rice until half done in lightly salted water, then drip dry.

To prepare the stuffing: put the ground meat in a bowl and add the egg, the pre-cooked rice and the finely chopped onion sautéed in the oil until transparent. Season with salt, pepper, and some of the finely chopped parsley. Combine thoroughly. Stuff the kohlrabi with this mixture. If any stuffing is left, shape into small balls.

Place the stuffed kohlrabi in a deep fireproof dish, surround with the cut-up pieces of kohlrabi and the extra meat balls. Add just enough water to cover the kohlrabi about a third of the way. Salt, cover, and cook over low heat until tender. When done, lift out the kohlrabi with a slotted spoon, set aside, and keep warm.

Mix together 2–3 tbsp. of the sour cream with the flour until smooth, add a little water, and stir again. Stir into the kohlrabi juice and bring to the boil. Place the stuffed kohlrabi back in the dish, sprinkle with the remaining parsley and a bit of the left-over sour cream. Serve the rest of the sour cream in a separate dish.

Paprika potatoes

(Paprikáskrumpli)

5 oz. smoked bacon	*2¼ lb. potatoes*
1 large onion	*1 tomato*
1 green pepper	*salt*
5 oz. paprika sausage	*pepper*
1 heaped tsp. paprika	*generous pinch of ground cumin*

Fry the diced smoked bacon until most of the fat is rendered, sauté the finely chopped onion in the fat until transparent, add the green pepper cut into chunks, the paprika sausage cut into rings, and stew for a short time. Sprinkle with paprika, add the peeled potatoes cut into chunks or julienne slices, the tomatoes, skinned and quartered, salt and pepper to taste, and cook in the bacon fat for a minute or two, stirring all the time. Add just enough water to cover half-way, then cook, covered, over medium heat until all the ingredients are tender.

Note: To make this dish even more substantial, add plain or spicy frankfurters, but be sure it's not too watery, because it will lose flavor. The cumin is optional, but to add "bite" to this dish, make it with one or two strong green peppers, or serve them in a separate dish.

Mushroom stew

(Gombapörkölt)

2 lbs. mushrooms	*salt*
2 tbsp. oil	*pepper*
1 onion	*1 green pepper*
1 tsp. paprika	*1 tomato*

Clean and slice the mushrooms. Sauté the finely chopped onion in the oil until transparent. Remove from the stove, sprinkle with paprika, put back on the stove, add the mushrooms cut into thick slices or large chunks, salt and pepper to taste, add the green pepper cut into rings and the skinned and quartered tomatoes, cover and stew in its own juices over low heat. When nearly done, remove the lid and continue cooking until most of the cooking juice has evaporated. Serve with *galuska* dumplings *(see Chicken paprikás recipe)* or boiled potatoes.

Note: If you add sour cream to this dish towards the end of the cooking time, it becomes another Hungarian favorite, mushroom paprikás.

Sholet Hungarian style

(Sólet magyarosan)

1 1/4 lbs. large pinto beans	pepper
2 tbsp. oil or goose fat	6–8 eggs
1 large onion	1 lb. smoked meat (breast of duck or goose, pork knuckles, brisket of beef)
3 cloves garlic	
1 tbsp. flour	1 lb. unsmoked meat (tasty beef, pork, goose)
1 tsp. paprika	
salt	

51

Soak the beans in water overnight. Sauté the finely chopped onion in the fat until transparent. (Use a traditional, heavy pot!) Add the crushed garlic, the flour mixed into the paprika, stir and cook for a minute or two, add 1/2 qt. cold water, stir thoroughly, add the beans, the meat, and salt to taste. (Don't forget that the smoked meat contains salt.) Add a bit of pepper and enough water to cover. Bring to the boil, cover, and bake in a medium-hot oven for 3 to 4 hours. Check from time to time, adding a little water as needed, but make sure the beans will not be too watery. Do not stir while baking, just shake the pot. 20 to 25 minutes before the beans are ready, add 6-8 thoroughly washed raw eggs. When serving, place the sliced meats and sliced eggs on top of the beans.

Note: Sholet can be made from many kinds of meat as long as half of the meat is smoked. For extra taste, add some spicy sausage rings while the beans are cooking.

Layered potato casserole   6 servings

(Rakott burgonya)

21/4 lbs. potatoes (the type suitable for cooking)	*4 oz. butter or margarine*
	11/2 cups sour cream
6 hard-boiled eggs	*7 oz. smoked bacon*
7 oz. smoked, spicy sausage	*salt*

Start cooking the potatoes in their skins under cover in lightly salted water.

Meanwhile cut the sausage and hard-boiled eggs into rings, and the bacon into thin slices. When the potatoes are half done, drain, let cool, peel and cut into rings thick enough so they won't break when handled.

Butter the bottom and sides of a fireproof dish, lay half the bacon on the bottom followed by a layer of lightly salted potato rings (about 1/3 of the potatoes), then the sausage rings, the hard-boiled egg rings, sprinkle a bit of butter on top and a liberal amount of sour cream. Continue layering the dish in this order until all the ingredients are used up. Finish with a layer of potatoes. Cover with a layer of bacon and sprinkle with the left-over sour cream. Bake, covered, in a pre-heated oven for 25 to 30 minutes, remove the lid, and bake until the top is red and crisp.

Note: If you don't like to use bacon, you can leave it out, adding more butter or margarin instead to prevent the layered potatoes from being dry.

Also, if you like vegetables, you can add green pepper rings and tomatoes for layering.

If you are watching your diet, you can also substitute bologna, hot dog slices or thin precooked chicken slices for sausage, and kefir (if available in your territory) for the sour cream.

Vegetarians leave the meat out altogether and make this dish with sliced mushrooms and apples.

Layered potato casserole

Lecsó

2 lb. green peppers	5 oz. paprika sausage
1/2 lb. tomatoes	salt
7 oz. smoked bacon	1 heaping tsp. paprika
1 large onion	

Wash and core the green peppers and cut into rings. Blanche the tomatoes, peel and quarter. Render the thinly sliced smoked bacon until the fat comes out, then sauté the finely chopped onion in the lard until transparent. Add the green peppers, the paprika sausage cut into rings, and cook for 10 minutes. Add the tomatoes, salt to taste, sprinkle with paprika and cook, covered, over medium heat until the vegetables are tender, but not mushy.

Serve with sliced hot peppers in a separate dish for those who like this dish very hot.

Note: You can substitute 2 tbsp. oil for the smoked bacon, or add plain or spicy frankfurters to the sausage to enrich the taste. For those who like their food "hot", serve strong green peppers or crushed dried paprika in a separate bowl.

Pastas, Pastries & Sweets

Cottage cheese dumplings

(Túrógombóc)

1 1/4 lb. dry cottage cheese, pot cheese or farmer's cheese	*4 oz. butter*
	4 oz. bread crumbs
3 eggs, salt	*1 1/2 cups sour cream*
5 oz. semolina	*powdered sugar*

Put the cheese through a sieve. Combine with the eggs, the semolina, 1 tsp. melted butter, salt, and let stand for at least an hour. Wet your hands and shape the cheese mixture into small dumplings (appr. 1 tbsp. per dumpling), and cook in plenty of boiling, lightly salted water for 15 to 20 minutes. Because semolina is different in every country, test-cook one dumpling first. If the dumpling is too soft, add a bit more semolina to the mixture, if too hard, more cheese. Meanwhile, in a fireproof dish fry the bread crumbs in the butter until golden brown, add the cheese dumplings, and turn carefully until they are covered with the bread crumbs. Sprinkle with half of the sour cream. Serve the other half of the sour cream and the powdered sugar separately.

Note: If you decide not to use bread crumbs, sprinkle the dumplings with hot sour cream to which a bit of butter and sugar have been added.

Vargabéles

2 packets (8 pcs.) strudel dough	*4 oz. butter*
bread crumbs	*4 eggs*
for the stuffing: 10–12 oz. thin pasta	*1 lb. cottage cheese*
	1 1/2–2 cups sour cream
5 oz. powdered sugar	*grated peel of 1 lemon*
2 oz. vanilla sugar	*4 oz. raisins*

Cook the pasta in plenty of lightly salted water until half done. Meanwhile, whip up the egg yolks with the powdered sugar and half of the vanilla sugar, add the

crumbled up cottage cheese, the sour cream, the ground lemon peel and the raisins (soaked in lukewarm water).

Combine the well-drained noodles with the cottage cheese mixture, whip up the egg whites until stiff, and gently stir into the pasta and cottage cheese mix.

Butter a deep fireproof dish and line with 4 strudel doughs laid on top of each other, with some melted butter sprinkled on each layer, to prevent them from sticking together. Sprinkle lightly with bread crumbs, add the pasta and cottage cheese mix, and cover with the remaining 4 strudel doughs as before. Spread a bit of melted butter on top and bake in a pre-heated medium oven until crisp and golden brown (appr. 25 to 30 minutes). Let cool, cut into big portion-size squares, and serve with vanilla sugar sprinkled on the top.

Cottage cheese noodles

(Túrós csusza)

1 lb. flat noodles	*2 cups sour cream*
4 oz. smoked bacon	*10–12 oz. cottage cheese*

Cook the noodles in plenty of lightly salted boiling water, then drain thoroughly. Meanwhile, in a fireproof dish fry the smoked bacon, cut into small cubes, until brown, take out the small cracklings with a slotted spoon, set aside and keep warm. Stir 1 cup sour cream into the rendered bacon fat, add the cooked noodles, stir until well combined, crumble the cottage cheese on top, sprinkle with 1/2 cup sour cream, and top with the left-over cottage cheese and the bacon cracklings. Place in a pre-heated oven, heat until the top is crispy brown, and serve at once. Serve the remaining sour cream in a separate dish.

Plum dumplings

(Szilvás gombóc)

For the dumplings:
1 1/4 lb. potatoes
1 1/4 lb. plums
2 tbsp. cinnamon sugar
appr. 8 oz. flour
1 clump butter

1 egg
salt

For the fried bread crumbs:
2 tbsp. oil or 2 oz. butter
4 oz. bread crumbs
1 tbsp. powdered sugar

Cook the thoroughly cleaned potatoes in their skins and peel while still hot. Slit open the plums and remove the pits. If the plums are not sweet enough, place a bit of sugar or cinnamon sugar inside.

Rice the cooked potatoes, place in a large bowl, add the flour, the butter, the egg, and salt to taste. (Add enough flour to make a light but not runny dough.) Stretch the

dough out to 1/2 in. thickness on a floured board, then cut into 3 in. squares. Place a plum in the middle of each square, flour your hands, pull the corners together, and shape into small dumplings, making sure that each plum is completely covered, and the dumplings will not fall apart while cooking. Cook in ample boiling water until the dumplings rise to the surface, then continue cooking for another 2 to 3 minutes. Remove immediately with a slotted spoon.

Brown the bread crumbs lightly in the butter, place the dumplings carefully on top of the bread crumbs, and carefully roll round to coat. Remove the dumplings and serve sprinkled with powdered sugar.

Note: These dumplings can also be made with prune jam, apricots or sweet greengages.

Walnut and poppy-seed rolls — 6–8 servings (2 rolls)
(Diós és mákos beigli)

For the pastry:
  1 lb. flour
  8–9 oz. butter or margarine
  3 eggs, salt
  3/4 oz. yeast
  1 tbsp. powdered sugar
  2/3 cups sour cream
  powdered sugar for sprinkling
For the walnut filling:
  10–11 oz. ground walnuts
  7 oz. sugar
  1/2 cup milk and water mixture
  1 small stick vanilla
  1 tsp. grated lemon peel

  2 oz. raisins soaked in water or rum
For the poppy-seed filling:
  8–9 oz. ground poppy-seed
  7 oz. sugar
  juice and grated peel of 1 lemon
  1 tbsp. butter
  1/4 cup milk and water mixture
  2 oz. raisins soaked in water or rum
  1 grated apple
For baking:
  flour
  2 eggs

To prepare the dough: combine the flour with the crumbled butter or margarine. Crumble the yeast into the warmed up milk to which sugar has been added. Wait until it rises (2 to 3 minutes), add the flour, the eggs, the sour cream, salt to taste and work together thoroughly to obtain a medium-stiff dough. Divide into two or four loaves and refrigerate for at least 3 to 4 hours.

To prepare the filling: add the sugar to the milk and water mixture, bring to a boil, add the rest of the ingredients, and cook over low heat, stirring constantly, for appr. 10 minutes. (When making the poppy-seed filling, add the grated apple only 2 to 3 minutes before the filling is ready.)

Roll out each clump of dough into a square and sprinkle with the cooled-down filling, leaving about an inch free around the edge. Gently roll up, pressing the two ends together with your fingers. Place on a buttered and floured baking tin, baste the top with the egg yolk, let stand for a while, then baste with the whites of 2 egg. After a couple of minutes, pierce the rolls with a small meat skewer or pin to prevent the dough from splitting, and bake in a pre-heated medium oven for appr. 35 to 40 minutes or until golden brown. Let cool on the baking tin, then carefully remove and cut into finger-thick slices. Serve sprinkled with powdered sugar.

Strudel with walnuts and morello cherries

(Diós és meggyes rétes)   8–10 servings

4 packets strudel dough
(2 sheets to a packet)

5 oz. butter

For the walnut filling:

1 1/2 cups milk

8–9 oz. ground walnuts

5 oz. vanilla sugar

4 oz. raisins soaked in milk

1 tsp. grated lemon peel

1 clump butter

For the morello cherry filling:

1 1/4 lb. morello cherries

14 oz. powdered sugar

4 oz. grated walnuts

1/2 tsp. grated lemon peel

ground cinnamon

1/2 tsp. powdered cinnamon

2 oz. bread crumbs

*Strudel with walnuts and
morello cherries*

To prepare the walnut filling: Bring the milk to the boil, add the ground walnuts, the powdered sugar, the raisins, the ground lemon peel and the small knob of butter. When the milk comes to the boil once again, remove from the fire and let cool. To prepare the morello cherry filling: Pit the cherries, let drain, combine with the powdered sugar, the ground walnuts, the lemon peel, and some cinnamon.

Carefully roll out the strudel sheets on a dishcloth (use 4 sheets per strudel), sprinkle the top of each with melted butter and breadcrumbs, sprinkle 1/3 of the surface lengthwise with half of the stuffing, and with the help of the dishcloth, roll up, but not too tightly, as the dough will expand. Proceed the same way to stuff the rest of the strudel sheets.

Place two of the strudel rolls on a well buttered baking sheet, brush the surface with melted butter, and bake in a pre-heated medium oven for 20–25 minutes or until golden brown and crisp. Remove from the oven and dust with powdered sugar. Proceed the same way with the other two studle rolls.

Tip: For a delightful variety, you can substitute sugared poppy seeds for the walnuts and cherries for the morello cherries, but in that case, use less sugar. You can also make strudel with apple, cottage cheese or cabbage filling.

Somlói galuska   6–8 servings

4 oz. raisins soaked in rum	For the vanilla cream:
4 oz. ground walnuts	*1 1/2 cups milk*
whipped cream made from 1 cup heavy cream	*1 vanilla pod*
	3 egg yolks
For the sponge cake:	*3 oz. sugar*
6 eggs	*1 tsp. cornstarch*
6 tbsp. powdered sugar	For the chocolate syrup:
6 tbsp. flour	*7 oz. bitter dark chocolate*
4 oz. walnuts	*2/3 cup milk or heavy cream*
1 heaping tbsp. cocoa	*2 tbsp. rum*
For the rum sauce:	For decorating:
1 cup water, 5 oz. sugar	*whipped cream made from 1 cup heavy cream*
1 tsp. grated lemon peel	
1 tsp. grated orange peel	
2 tbsp. rum	

To prepare the sponge cake: beat the egg yolks and sugar until stiff, add the flour, then the stiffly beaten egg whites. Divide the mixture into three portions. Fold the grated walnuts into one, the cocoa into the other, and leave the third portion plain. Pour one mixture at a time into a baking tin lined with baking paper (about the thickness of a finger) and bake in a pre-heated medium over. (The sponge cake takes

about 12 minutes to bake, so do not open the oven door, otherwise the cake will collapse.) To prepare the vanilla cream: boil the milk with the vanilla pod for 5 minutes and remove from the fire. Mix the egg yolks, the sugar and cornstarch thoroughly together and add to the hot milk.

To prepare the rum sauce: cook the sugar, the lemon and orange peel in 1 cup of water for 15 minutes. Let cool and add the rum.

For the chocolate sauce: melt the chocolate, broken into bits, over a low flame in 2/3 cup milk or heavy cream, stir in the rum, and let cool.

Break the three kinds of sponge cake into smaller pieces and combine. Place a layer of sponge cake in the bottom of a large glass dish. Sprinkle with the rum sauce, the grated walnut, the raisin, smooth a portion of the vanilla cream on top, then repeat this procedure until all the ingredients have been used up, but reserve some sponge cake for the top. Sprinkle with cocoa, cover with the whipped cream, and sprinkle the chocolate sauce over the whipped cream.

Note: This delicacy can also be made from store-bought sponge cake.

Gundel pancakes   10–12 pancakes

(Gundel palacsinta)

10–12 pancakes *(see Hortobágy pancakes recipe)*

For the filling:

1/2 cup heavy cream	31/2 – 4 oz. powdered sugar
5 oz. ground walnuts	2 oz. raisins soaked in rum
	1 tsp. candied orange peel

For the chocolate sauce:

1 cup milk	*1 tbsp. vanilla sugar*
1 cup heavy cream	*1 tbsp. rum*
5 oz. chocolate	*3 egg yolks*
1 tbsp. melted butter	*2 oz. sugar*

Prepare the pancakes and stack on a plate.

To prepare the filling: bring the heavy cream to the boil over low heat, add the ground walnuts, the powdered sugar, the raisins soaked in rum, the candied orange peel cut into very thin strips, and boil for 1 minute. Let cool a bit, pile a heaping tbsp. of filling in the middle of each pancake and fold over the four sides or roll up. Place in a fireproof dish and keep warm.

To prepare the chocolate sauce: whip up the egg yolks and the sugar until frothy. Place the crumbled up chocolate in the milk and melt over low heat, then add the butter, the vanilla sugar, and the rum. Stirring constantly, pour into the egg yolk mixture and reheat, but make sure the mixture does not come to a boil! (If the sauce is not thick enough, add a bit of cornstarch.) Remove from the heat, whip up the heavy cream until stiff and carefully fold into the sauce. Pour the sauce over the pancakes and serve piping hot.

Gundel pancakes

Contents

Poultry and Meats 27

Stuffed chicken 27
  Töltött csirke
Chicken paprikás with galuska dumplings 29
  Paprikáscsirke galuskával
Chicken legs with grapes 29
  Szőlős csirkecombok
Goose giblets with rice 31
  Rizses libaaprólék
Ground breast of goose 31
  Vagdalt libamell
Stuffed turkey breast Bakony style 32
  Bakonyi töltött pulykamell
Veal pörkölt 32
  Borjúpörkölt
Veal medallions in white wine 34
  Részeges borjútokány
Stuffed breast of veal 34
  Töltött borjúszegy
Hungarian escalopes of veal 35
  Magyaros bélszínérmék
Veal stew in red wine 36
  Vörösboros marhapörkölt
Escalopes of veal Budapest style 36
  Bélszín Budapest módra
Pan-fried rostélyos 37
  Serpenyős rostélyos
Roast suckling pig with stewed cabbage 38
  Malacsült párolt káposztával
Knuckle of ham Hungarian style 39
  Csülök pékné módra
Pork with potatoes 39
  Brassói aprópecsenye
Csabai pork chops 40
  Csabai sertéskaraj
Csikós tokány 40
  Csikós tokány
Vasi pecsenye 42
  Vasi pecsenye
Transylvanian mixed grill 42
  Erdélyi fatányéros
Pork with mushrooms 43
  Gombás flekken

Highwayman's treat on a spit 44
  Rablóhús nyárson
Braised liver 44
  Pirított máj

Casseroles 45

Stuffed cabbage 45
  Töltött káposzta
Stuffed peppers 46
  Töltött paprika
Layered Savoy cabbage 47
  Rakott kel
Stuffed squash with dill sauce 48
  Töltött tök kapormártással
Stuffed kohlrabi 49
  Töltött karalábé
Paprika potatoes 50
  Paprikáskrumpli
Mushroom stew 50
  Gombapörkölt
Sholet Hungarian style 51
  Sólet magyarosan
Layered potato casserole 52
  Rakott burgonya
Lecsó 54
  Lecsó

Pastas, Pastries & Sweets 55

Cottage cheese dumplings 55
  Túrógombóc 55
Vargabéles 55
  Vargabéles
Cottage cheese noodles 56
  Túrós csusza 56
Plum dumplings 57
  Szilvás gombóc 57
Walnut and poppy-seed rolls 58
  Diós és mákos beigli 58
Strudel with walnuts and morello cherries 59
  Diós és meggyes rétes 59
Somlói galuska 60
  Somlói galuska 60
Gundel pancakes 61
  Gundel palacsinta 61